THE HIST
SCHOOLS' RUGBY LEAGUE
IN LEEDS

THE HISTORY OF SCHOOLS' RUGBY LEAGUE IN LEEDS

Steve Boothroyd

Scratching Shed Publishing Ltd

A catalogue record for this book is available from the
British Library.

Typeset in Warnock Pro Semi Bold and Palatino
Printed and bound in the United Kingdom by
Page Bros (Norwich) Ltd
Mile Cross Lane, Norwich, Norfolk NR6 6SA
Telephone 01603 778800

For all those people who have played a part – as players, supporters, coaches, referees and administrators – in the history of schools' rugby league in Leeds.

Contents

1.
The Early Years
1902-1916

The Beginning

Research suggests that Leeds Grammar School was the first school in Leeds to play rugby, perhaps as early as the 1850s.

Matches were played by a mixture of pupils and masters, mainly against club sides, although there is evidence of a schools' Challenge Cup from 1888. The school found it difficult to arrange matches against neighbouring schools and fixtures dried up after a while due to the lack of top level local rugby union sides to act as role models, plus the apathy of pupils and parents. When the school started playing again in the 20th century it was most certainly allied to the 'old' RUGBY union, as opposed to the 'new' NORTHERN Union.

The first city-wide association to be organised in Leeds, while called the *Leeds Schools' Rugby Football Union*, was certainly allied to the Northern Union, as early trophies were donated by the Hunslet and Leeds clubs and matches were staged at Parkside and Headingley.

The association's first annual general meeting was held at the Green Dragon Hotel (off the Headrow, Green Dragon Yard still exists) on 3rd September 1903. The minutes record that 24 gentlemen attended and that: *...it was resolved to issue a printed circular to the public for subscriptions towards a fund for providing trophies and medals.*

The first chairman was Thomas Vernon Harrison (then a teacher, at Christ Church School in Hunslet, who first proposed Children's Day at Roundhay Park and after whom the sports' ground on Oldfield Lane was named).

One of the other officials of the new association was Mr J R H 'Bert' Greaves, who confirmed in the *Jubilee Handbook* of 1952 that he was one of 18 gentlemen who met in 1902 to form the association. Another prominent official from this era was James Lyon, who served as treasurer for over 30 years – a feat surpassed only by the association's current treasurer, Peter Woodhead.

In the first season (1902-03) a knockout cup and 'friendlies' were played at 15-a-side, mirroring Northern Union rules. At the first AGM it was agreed to run a league competition and rules were changed so that matches would be played 12-a-side, pre-dating the Northern Union's reduction to 13-a-side by two years. Matches were played at Under 13 age-level, to reflect the school leaving age for most pupils in those days.

Goldthorpe Cup

It is thought that the Goldthorpe Cup is the oldest trophy still being competed for in schools' rugby league. The minutes of 15th January 1904 record that: *Mr T V Harrison, on behalf of the Hunslet Cricket Football and Athletic Club, presented to the Schools' Union the handsome Goldthorpe Trophy.*

On 19th February, it was unanimously agreed that: *The Goldthorpe Trophy be the challenge cup of the Union*, and a draw featuring 23 teams was made.

The eventual winners were Bramley National (now Bramley St Peter's) who beat Burley Lawn (closed in the 1960s, but at that time on the corner of Cardigan Road and Burley Road).The final was at Parkside, with Albert and Walter Goldthorpe (two members of the legendary family, after whom the trophy was named) being asked to act as touch judges. As Albert Goldthorpe was perhaps the greatest player of his generation, this would seem nowadays to be an unbelievable match official appointment. Furthermore, Albert's wife Jane presented the trophy.

The *LSRFU Handbook* of 1908-09 lists Hunslet Carr as winners of the Goldthorpe Cup in 1902-03, beating Jack Lane in the final. Presumably, however, this was a retrospective honour.

League Championship

At the first AGM it was resolved that: *the city be divided into three districts, North South and East, and that the championship of the city be decided by the top school of each district playing the top school of each of the other districts one match on neutral ground.*

The first winners of the league championship were Bramley National, which meant they completed the 'double' in 1903-04. Reflecting on the achievement, their coach, Mr Greaves, recalled: *What a Bramley welcome greeted the team on their return to 'The Village' – the horse-drawn wagonettes were met by the Bramley Brass Band and escorted up the crowded Town Street!*

Bramley went on to win the league championship on a further six occasions before competitions were disbanded in

1916 due to the First World War. Other schools to be crowned league champions in this era were Burley Lawn and Jack Lane (twice each) and Bewerley Street and Halton (once each). The Leeds club had donated a trophy for this competition. In early documents it was known as the Leeds FC Shield; from 1913 it was known as the Sheldon Shield. The Wynne Trophy (donated by the family in memory of Richard Wynne, a headmaster in Hunslet) was first presented in 1911-1912 as a knockout trophy for senior sides – excluding top teams – and then used as a League 2 champions trophy.

Yorkshire Cup

The fact that a Yorkshire Cup Competition also began in 1903-04, suggests that organised schools' rugby was taking place in other towns and cities at this time too.

Wakefield schools triumphed on the first two occasions (Outwood Church School followed by Loscoe Council School). The coming three years saw St Mary's of Bradford complete a hat-trick. After which, Leeds schools came to dominate the final. Bramley National (1907) and Bewerley Street (1908) were runners-up before the city provided both finalists in 1909, with St Hilda's beating Bramley, and in 1910, Bramley beating Burley Lawn. Jack Lane were runners-up in 1911, with Bramley winning again in 1912 and finishing as runners-up in 1914.

Representative Teams

From the start of the 1903-04 season, teacher-coaches were selecting representative teams to play in fixtures such as: North v South, Reds v Stripes, Possibles v Probables, Leeds Boys v Hunslet Boys, Hunslet Boys v Bramley Boys, League

Winners v The Rest. The first match against another union was played at the Park Avenue ground, against Bradford, on Saturday 31st October 1903. The team colours were green and black. The following boys formed the squad:

Back: Tattersdale (Jack Lane). Threequarters: Hartley (Cockburn), Lister and Tyndall (Bramley). Halves: Cobham (Bramley) and Sheldon (Hunslet Carr). Forwards: Wood and Lawrence (Bramley), Waterworth (Beeston Hill), Stead (Jack Lane), Hodge (Park Lane) and Dixon (Hunslet Carr). Reserves: Turner (Ellerby Lane), Poulter (Park Lane), Lamb (Jack Lane) and Bielby (Low Road).

Their next matches were played at Hull and Oldham where: *After the match both teams will have tea at the Derker Board School, which will be followed by a cinematograph entertainment.* The first home match was played on the Barley Mow Ground, Bramley, on Saturday 13th February 1904 against Barrow, with the following arrangements made: *10.50am, Barrow team arrive; 12.30pm, dinner at Co-operative Restaurant, Albion Street; 3pm, kick off; 6pm, tea and meeting in restaurant; 10.55pm, visitors leave Leeds.* The City team played matches at Headingley and Parkside during the following seasons and also met teams from Huddersfield, Dewsbury & Batley, Wakefield and Halifax.

In 1909-10 the Leeds City Boys, captained by Cliff Pepper of Bramley National School, won the Yorkshire Schools' Shield as inter-city Champions. It would be almost 40 years before this honour was won again.

The meeting of 16th January 1916 was the last of the LSRFU until after the First World War. The league champions (Bramley) had been determined from matches played during the first part of the campaign. It was decided that the Goldthorpe Cup competition would not take place. Engraving on the Sheldon Shield shows the Bramley captain for 1915-16 as Harold Edmondson, who, three years later on 1st February 1919, would become the youngest-ever professional player when he made his debut for Bramley against Bradford Northern, aged 15 years and 81 days.

2.
The Inter-War Years
1919-1939

After the First World War, a 'Reorganising Meeting' of the Leeds Schools' Rugby Football Union was held in the Headingley Pavilion, on Friday 12th September 1919. The season was soon in full swing and by the end there was a new name on the honours board, with Blenheim proving to be the outstanding team by winning the Sheldon Shield and the Goldthorpe Cup.

Hunslet Carr's Dynasty

The 1920-21 season saw the start of an amazing run of success by the Hunslet Carr school. They were undefeated over five years and during this time won 148 out of 150 games, scoring 5,931 points (an average of well over 40 a game). After completing 100 successive wins, in March 1924 it was reported that local Hunslet people had presented the school with a gramophone. The teacher-coach throughout this period of success was Mr G H Cripps.

The breakdown below shows that 1920-21 was a slow start to the dynasty. Two matches were drawn and only 306 points scored. However in the four years after that the school built up a phenomenal record:-

Season	P	W	D	L	Points for	Points against
1920-21	29	27	2	0	306	14
1921-22	25	25	0	0	1,157	6
1922-23	36	36	0	0	1,840	36
1923-24	32	32	0	0	1,588	35
1924-25	28	28	0	0	1,040	3
	150	148	2	0	5,931	94

For five successive seasons they completed a treble of League Champions, Goldthorpe Cup and Yorkshire Cup. Hunslet Carr enjoyed another period of success in the late 1920s/early 1930s, winning the Goldthorpe Cup for another five consecutive seasons from 1927-28 to 1931-32. Other strong Hunslet teams in this era were Jack Lane, Hunslet National and Middleton, who emerged as Hunslet Champions for the four years leading up to the war.

Hunslet Break Away

On Wednesday 8th June 1921 a meeting was held at Parkside and a unanimous decision taken: *That a Hunslet Schools Rugby Union be formed for the purpose of encouraging the playing of Rugby Football amongst the schoolboys of Hunslet.*

The new association's first chairman was Mr T V Harrison, who had been the first chairman of the Leeds association 18 years earlier, and a trophy was purchased for winners of the Senior League, named the T V Harrison Shield in his honour. Councillor W H 'Billy' Gilston, a founder and captain of the Hunslet club in 1883, presented a cup, used initially for a knockout competition but later for the winners of the Junior League (what would now be called League 2).

The Hunslet club donated a trophy, the Lewthwaite Cup (named after Hunslet president Joe Lewthwaite), for winners of a knockout competition.

While another trophy, known as the Cripps Cup after the Hunslet Schools' RU secretary and above-mentioned Hunslet Carr teacher-coach, was competed for by school 'A' teams (second teams) and also by League 2 and 3 sides. There was disagreement over the Goldthorpe Cup: the Leeds Union said it should be theirs, as it had been presented to their association; the Hunslet Union said it should be theirs, as it had been presented by the Hunslet Club.

The matter was finally resolved when the cup became the property of the Hunslet Union in 1925. During this period, a number of schools fielded 'A' teams and some even 'B' and 'C' teams. Leagues were organised on ability rather than age, all teams playing at Under 14, the new school leaving age.

The Hunslet association did organise an Under 11s league from 1937-38 but no trophies were awarded for this competition until after the war.

Meanwhile Back In Leeds

While the Leeds Union retained the Sheldon Shield for the winners of the Senior League, the association introduced a number of new trophies in the 1920s and 1930s.

The T H Wilson Cup (named after a Leeds RLFC director and local businessman) was the new knockout trophy. The Burton Cup (from the famous Leeds tailoring company), the Stephenson Cup (from the local department store of the same name) and the Jas Lyon Trophy (named after long-serving treasurer James Lyon, who passed away in 1932 while still in post) were all league trophies.

As with the Hunslet association, all trophies were competed for at Under 14, with a junior (Under 11) league introduced in 1934-35, but no trophy for the winners until after the war. At the 1921 AGM it was agreed that games should now be played at 13-a-side.

Schools from areas closest to the Leeds ground (Headingley, Burley, Woodhouse, Meanwood) dominated the main competition. Burley National and Quarry Mount were both league champions five times during this era, Buslingthorpe National three times, Meanwood Road and Brudenell once each, with 'outsiders' York Road and Bramley also winning once each.

Other teams amongst the honours were Cross Stamford Street, Woodhouse, Blenheim and Kirkstall Road. In addition, the Jas Wilson Cup (donated by James W Wilson, director of William Wilson & Sons Ltd, *perambulator and toy makers of Guiseley*, later to become Silver Cross) was first awarded in 1933 to the winners of a four-team play-off involving the two top sides from the Leeds and Hunslet leagues.

This was dominated by Hunslet sides during the first six years: Hunslet National and Middleton being outright winners twice each and Hunslet Carr sharing with Quarry Mount in 1935, while Middleton shared with Brudenell the following year.

Yorkshire Competitions

Again it was the Hunslet sides that enjoyed more success than Leeds sides in county competitions during the inter-war years. As well as their domination of the Yorkshire Cup in the early 1920s, Hunslet Carr were runners-up in later years, as were Jack Lane and Hunslet National, before Middleton won the Cup in 1938. The previous year had seen Buslingthorpe win the Cup after being runners-up in 1932; whilst Burley National were runners-up in 1931.

In 1930 the Hunslet City Boys won the Yorkshire Shield, beating Hull in the final at Parkside; Hunslet were champions again in 1931, 1936 and 1938. This was a barren period for Leeds city teams, but the balance of power was to shift after the Second World War.

The First Wembley Trip

In 1933 the Leeds and Hunslet associations combined to run the first ever schoolboy trip to Wembley.

Travelling by train to London, with a sightseeing omnibus trip around the capital, 436 boys and 44 adults saw Huddersfield beat Warrington in only the fourth Cup final to be staged at the national stadium.

With financial assistance from the *Yorkshire Evening Post* and Leeds MPs, the trip cost the boys the princely sum of 12 shillings (60p)!

In 1934 Hunslet schoolboys saw their favourites beat Widnes and in 1936 Leeds schoolboys saw their heroes beat Warrington. These trips were to continue for over 30 years.

With Britain at war again in 1939, school competitions and activities of both associations were suspended until 1946.

The History of Schools' RL in Leeds

Matches were played on an ad hoc basis, as noted by the following entry in the Hunslet Schools' minute book: *The War: A Break of 7 Years during which those teachers remaining carried on and kept rugby alive in South Leeds.*

Jack Lane – Goldthorpe Cup and Leeds FC Shield winners, 1906-07

Bramley National – Yorkshire Cup, Leeds FC Shield
and Goldthorpe Cup, 1909-10

Harold Edmondson (Bramley National) with the Sheldon Shield and the Wynne Trophy, 1915-16

Bob Lundy (Hunslet Carr) with the Yorkshire Cup, Gilston Cup and Goldthorpe Cup, 1921-22

Bramley National teacher-coach J R H 'Bert' Greaves

T V Harrison, the first chairman of LSRFU and later the first chairman of HSRFU

Hunslet Carr – Goldthorpe Cup, Yorkshire Cup
and Sheldon Shield winners, 1920-21

Cross
Stamford
Street –
1922-23

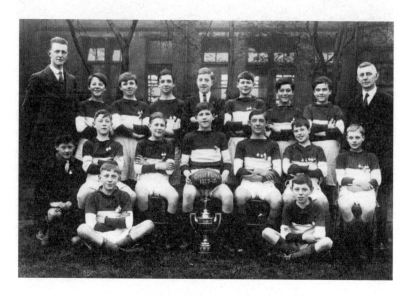

Cross Flatts Park – Gilston Cup winners, 1925-26

Buslingthorpe National – Burton Cup, Sheldon Shield
and T H Wilson Cup winners, 1932-33

Hunslet National – Jas Wilson Cup, T V Harrison Shield
and Goldthorpe Cup winners, 1932-33

Kirkstall Road – Burton Cup winners, 1933-34

Leeds City Boys – Yorkshire Champions, 1947-48
– with Leeds player Dickie Williams

Kirkstall Road – senior and intermediate teams, 1949-50 – winners of the
Greaves Trophy, Jas Wilson Cup, Burton Cup, Sheldon Shield,
Yorkshire Cup and TH Wilson Cup

St Simon's – Stephenson Cup winners, 1951-52

Leeds City Boys, 1951-52

Winning schools parade trophies at Headingley, 1953-54

St Joseph's – Goldthorpe Cup winners, 1954-55

3.
A Boom Era
1946-1960

The years after the Second World War saw a period of expansion and success for sport in general in Britain, despite austerity and rationing lingering for a few years after the conclusion of hostilities. The 1940s and 1950s certainly reflected the national profile and saw a boom era for shools' rugby league in Leeds.

The first meeting of the Leeds association after the war, was held on 12th February 1946, in the old Bowling Club at the Headingley ground, when *The members stood in silence as a token of respect for J H Stevenson, Master of Quarry Mount School, killed in action.* While at the first Hunslet Schools' meeting, on 1st July 1946, all the demobilised members were present and welcomed back. At both meetings arrangements were made to re-start competitions and grant applications were made.

At the Leeds meeting on 23rd September 1947 it was recorded that the association *had been allocated 370 clothing coupons ... to be allocated to schools according to number of teams playing rugby.*

More Teams and New Competitions

When competitions were fully up and running by 1947-48, the Leeds association had two senior leagues (now at Under 15, to mirror another new school leaving age), one second team league and one junior (Under 11) league. Intermediate leagues were soon introduced at Under 14 and Under 13, the number of junior teams increased significantly and by 1959-1960 there were three senior leagues, four intermediate leagues and four junior leagues.

New trophies introduced during this era were the Burton Trophy (a second cup donated by the famous local tailoring company), the Adams Award (named after Meanwood-born former Leeds player Les 'Juicy' Adams, who died in action during the war) and the Greaves and Park trophies (both of which were named after long-serving LSRL administrators).

Different names amongst the senior honours were Primrose Hill and Burmantofts, while a number of schools won trophies for the first time at intermediate level with the increased number of trophies available. The strong teams in the junior leagues included Quarry Mount, Kirkstall, Broad Lane and Alwoodley.

The Hunslet association also introduced an intermediate competition and increased to two junior leagues. Middleton and Belle Isle were the most successful junior sides. Immediately after the war, both the Leeds and Hunslet associations introduced trophies for junior competitions, re-allocating existing trophies: the Stephenson Trophy and the Cripps Cup.

Coaching Pioneers

As well as continuing to run trips to Wembley, the Hunslet and Leeds associations combined to form a joint *Sub-Committee on Coaching*. The initial idea was to formulate a coaching scheme, which involved 12 sessions of *lecture, demonstration, practice* leading to a diploma.

The schoolteachers involved were to work with the Rugby Football League and Mr S Shaw (chief organiser of physical education in Leeds). The aims were:

a. *To raise the standard of Rugby Football amongst schoolboys.*
b. *To produce a scheme that may be adopted by the Senior R.L. body.*
c. *To foster the spirit of sportsmanship.*

What developed from the first meeting on 16th November 1946 was much more than this. The planned sessions duly took place for the first time in June and July 1947, with 34 participants.

The committee then brought out a handbook *giving guidance and continuity to instructors*, first published in May 1948 as *Manual of Rugby League Coaching*. It was the first-ever coaching manual produced and for over 30 years remained the only such guide, until Ray French wrote *Coaching Rugby League* in 1982, soon followed by Phil Larder's *The Rugby League Skills Manual* in 1983 and *The Rugby League Coaching Manual* in 1988. Both gentlemen referenced the pioneering coaching handbook produced by the Leeds and Hunslet Schools' Rugby Leagues, which had been revised in 1950 and reprinted in 1971.

The History of Schools' RL in Leeds

While the rules of rugby league may have changed greatly since 1948, and sections such as *Scrummaging* have since become redundant, there are still many ideas contained within the book which could be useful today.

Leeds Teams Lead the Way

While the Hunslet area provided the best school teams in the years immediately before the Second World War, the early post-war years were dominated by Leeds schools.

Buslingthorpe National dominated senior and junior competitions in the first couple of years and then for the next four years Kirkstall held the Jas Wilson Cup – their first ever spell as city champions. For the first three of these seasons they were also Yorkshire champions.

Golden Jubilee

Leeds Schools' Rugby League celebrated its Golden Jubilee in style, with a presentation ceremony at the Headingley Pavilion in May 1953, attended by the Lord Mayor Alderman F B Burnley. Two founding members, vice-presidents Messrs G H Cripps and J R H Greaves, were present at the event; while two serving officials, Messrs H Bateson and G M Dorney, were amongst the speakers. The former is still remembered annually at the presentation of the Ben Bateson Award. The latter, Glynn Dorney, was a legend of schools' rugby league: attending his first meeting in 1930, he continued to be a regular at meetings until 1988. He oversaw successful junior teams at Bentley Lane and Alwoodley, as well as being treasurer of the association for 15 years.

Other well-respected officials were Bob Sheppard, who served as secretary for 14 years, Ken Dalby, who moved from coaching Kirkstall School to coaching the Leeds first team and writing histories of the Leeds club, and W H 'George' Hirst, who was elected a life member in 1957 and in 1963 became the first non-teacher chairman of LSRL; he also served as president and auditor for the association and in the professional rugby league world as Leeds secretary and Yorkshire secretary and treasurer.

The outstanding side in 1952-53 was Brudenell, who won the Leeds league and knockout trophies, were city champions and also won the Yorkshire Cup, beating Middleton in the final. In addition, the Leeds side captained by Meanwood's Fred Anderson won the Yorkshire Shield as inter-city champions. The intermediate champions were Buslingthorpe National and the junior champions were Burley National, with Sacred Heart taking the junior knockout cup.

Hunslet Strength

Hunslet school St Joseph's emerged as the outstanding side of the mid-1950s. For three seasons from 1953-54 they won the Hunslet league and cup competitions and were also city champions; for the last two of these years they were Yorkshire champions too, beating Blenheim in the 1955 final. Their coach was Joe Arnold, who had taken over as chairman of the Hunslet association in 1953 and was to remain in this post for over 25 years, before becoming president until the merger with Leeds in 1996.

Two other long-standing officials from this era were Edgar Meeks, who was amongst the founder members of the association in 1921 and served as treasurer, chairman and then president until his death in 1968, and Frank Sephton, who served as treasurer from 1932 until 1966; then less than a year after taking over as president he too passed away, in 1969. Subsequently the pavilion at the Arthur Thornton Sports Ground was named after these two stalwarts of Hunslet schools' rugby league.

Shared Success

Following the success of St Joseph's, the next four seasons saw the Jas Wilson Cup, for the city championship, shared equally between Leeds and Hunslet and four schools: Blenheim, Hunslet Carr, Brudenell and Middleton, who also ended the decade as Yorkshire champions.

The immediate post-war years saw the emergence of two teachers whose involvement in schools' rugby league spanned over 60 years, until they both passed away within a few months of each other in 2016.

The first was Harry Jepson: well-known for his involvement in the professional game, Harry was elected a life member and vice-president of the Hunslet association, after serving as secretary; he was then a vice-president of the combined Leeds & Hunslet SRL.

The second was Ron Pace, who also began his teaching career in Hunslet, but moved to Leeds where he was a city team coach, chairman, and then president of Leeds SRL and subsequently Leeds & Hunslet SRL for 25 years. Both gentlemen were stalwarts of the game and of course spent a number of years coaching rugby league in their own schools.

Yorkshire Champions

In an 11-year period, from 1947-48 to 1957-58, the Yorkshire Shield for the inter-city championship was won on nine occasions by Hunslet or Leeds.

Hunslet triumphed in 1952, 1955, 1956, 1957 and 1958, and were runners-up in 1948; while Leeds were victorious in 1948, 1950, 1953 and 1954, and were runners-up in 1949 and 1958. Such success consequently provided a number of boys who went on to star for the Hunslet and Leeds senior sides. The Leeds 1957 cup final side included Del Hodgkinson (Blenheim), Jeff Stevenson (Buslingthorpe), George Broughton (Bentley Lane) and Jack Lendill (Kirkstall), while another Kirkstall boy, Trevor Whitehead, played in the 1961 championship final. It was most fitting that Robin Dewhurst signed for Leeds, as he had starred for St Michael's C/E (the nearest junior school to Headingley) and Brudenell (the nearest senior school to Headingley), as well as captaining the City Boys team and Yorkshire Schoolboys in 1958-59.

Around the same time, future Leeds international winger John Atkinson was taking his first steps in rugby league at Iveson House Junior School. Hunslet Schoolboys comprised 13 of the 18 players in the Hunslet 1965 cup final squad: Geoff Gunney, Geoff Shelton, Billy Baldwinson and Ron Whittaker (Dewsbury Road), Billy Langton and Ken Eyre (Bewerley Street), Alan Preece and Barry Lee (Hunslet National), Bill Ramsey and Ray Abbey (Hunslet Carr), Brian Gabbitas (Cross Flatts Park), Bernard Prior (St Joseph's) and Arthur Render (Beeston). Eyre and Ramsey also played at Wembley for Leeds in 1968, along with other Hunslet Schoolboys Albert Eyre (Bewerley Street), Syd Hynes (Dewsbury Road), Mick Shoebottom (Low Road) and Barry Seabourne (Bewerley Street and Belle Isle).

Representative teams were introduced at intermediate (Under 13) level in 1950-51, but it would be more than 20 years before trophies were on offer at this age level.

4.
Continued Success in the City
1960-1972

Belle Isle Dominate

The start of the 1960s saw the start of a decade of unprecedented domination by new secondary school Belle Isle, in Hunslet and in the wider area of the city and county. They won the Harrison Shield for eight successive seasons, were city champions in seven of these; they won the Yorkshire Cup three times (1962, 1966 and 1969) and were runners-up twice (1964 and 1965). They may well have reached the county final in 1963, but the competition was cancelled due to the harsh winter. As well as monopolising the senior championship, they dominated the Lewthwaite senior knockout cup, the Under 13 Goldthorpe Cup and the Under 12 Meeks Shield; the Belle Isle 'B' team even won the Senior League B on two occasions. In 1961-62 the school won seven trophies in total and at the 1969 Hunslet SRL AGM it was reported that *Belle Isle had won every trophy possible, including the Yorkshire Cup.*

The coaches during this period of success, unparalleled since the Hunslet Carr dynasty of the 1920s, were George Cranage and Bill Crann, two of the most successful schools' rugby league coaches ever. George started his coaching career at St George's Junior School (on Burley Street); the school won its only trophies under his tutelage in 1956-57. After building formidable teams at Belle Isle, he enjoyed similar success at Cross Green and later at Clapgate. George also coached trophy winning senior city sides in Hunslet and Leeds, as well as coaching the Yorkshire side.

Bill Crann started his coaching at Middleton in the late 1950s, then, after a couple of years at Stainbeck, moved to Belle Isle in 1964, before returning, in 1970, to Middleton, which later became John Blenkinsop Middle School. He finished his coaching career at Shakespeare in the mid-1980s. As well as being a successful coach, Bill also refereed schools games at the highest level and was a respected official in the professional game.

By the start of the 1970s, Belle Isle had been replaced by Parkside as the top Hunslet senior school, but they still managed another Yorkshire Cup final, as runners-up in 1971, before becoming a middle school just over a year later.

Other Hunslet Triumphs

The strength of the players and coaches at Belle Isle influenced the success of the Hunslet senior city side that completed a hat-trick of Yorkshire Shield triumphs from 1961-1962 to 1963-64. In each of these three years they provided the Yorkshire Schools' captain: Barry Seabourne and Alan Lamond (both Belle Isle) and Steven Lee (Hunslet C/E). In 1962 the senior Hunslet SRL side played against Hull in a curtain-raiser to the Yorkshire Cup final at Headingley between Hull KR and Hunslet. The intermediate city team was unbeaten in 1961-62.

In the domestic competitions St Joseph's and Middleton picked up a few trophies, but the team to emerge at the end of this era was Parkside, who picked up a hat-trick of senior league and cup victories (at Under 15 and Under 14), as well as lifting the Under 13 and Under 12 cups on two occasions. Heading the Parkside coaching team was Ken Bond, who coached the school's sides for 20 years and also coached the city intermediate and then senior sides during this time too. He was treasurer of the association from 1967 until the merger with Leeds in 1996.

A meeting of the Hunslet SRL on 22nd September 1965 reported *a drastic reduction in teams*, which saw senior schools arranging fixtures against Leeds schools while still maintaining two or three-team leagues in the south of the city. Finally, in 1967-68, Hunslet senior leagues were abandoned and all Hunslet senior sides played in the Leeds leagues.

The Hunslet association continued to organise its own senior and intermediate knockout cups, as well as a junior league for the Cripps Cup and from 1968-69 a junior knockout cup for the Pease Rose Bowl. In addition the first Clapgate 'Sevens' tournament was organised in 1971-72; continuing over 30 years. Cross Flatts was the most successful junior school at the start of this era and Clapgate the most successful at the end, while Bewerley Street and Hunslet Carr picked up their first trophies as junior schools.

Leeds Honours Spread

The start of the 1960s saw the familiar names of Kirkstall, Blenheim, Brudenell and Harehills on the senior honours board, along with a rare appearance for Osmondthorpe. This decade then saw the emergence of the 'new' comprehensive schools in the city; the Leeds association was determined to promote the playing of rugby league over rugby union in these establishments, and two such schools, Stainbeck and Cross Green, found success at senior and intermediate levels.

Other new names on trophies included St John Bosco and Abbey Grange, while Intake won more intermediate (Under 12 and 13) trophies than any other school. Altogether 20 different Leeds senior schools won trophies during this era. This spread of talent probably worked against Leeds: It was noted by chairman Chris Allison at the 1963 Leeds SRL AGM that: *One feature of City matches was the superiority of Hunslet teams.* While City team coach Harry Lamb *pointed out that the strength of Hunslet lay in their selection from 2 big schools.*

Nevertheless in 1963-64 the Leeds city senior team won the Yorkshire seven-a-side competition and were runners-up in the Yorkshire Shield. The city had one of the decade's outstanding schoolboys in John Holmes, who captained Kirkstall, Leeds and Yorkshire.

The Rise of the Junior Schools

As well as the healthy Hunslet Junior School League, Leeds SRL ran four or five junior leagues in most seasons during the 1960s and early 1970s. The standard of play improved and trophies were won by teams from all areas of the city, from Rodley in the west to Halton Moor in the east. The top schools still competed in a league for the Stephenson Cup, while the Hirst, Long and Headingley Cups were added to existing trophies.

Quarry Mount won the Stephenson Cup for a third time in four seasons in 1961-62, Alwoodley then won it three times in four years, before Queen's Road completed their own hat-trick, starting at the end of the decade. Broad Lane (twice), Bramley C/E and Sacred Heart were also champions during this era, while Bentley Lane and Iveson House won the Watson Trophy (the knockout cup for the top two leagues). Altogether 21 different schools won junior school league or cup honours during this period.

The Reg Watson Trophy began life as an Under 13 league trophy in 1959-60; in 1962-63 it became the Under 11 knockout cup, as it still is today. It was the first of four trophies to be donated by the Leeds RL Supporters' Social Club.

ESRL – A National Schools' Body for the Game

Although the first Yorkshire Cup competition was played in 1904, the Yorkshire SRL wasn't established as an official body until 1946, well after the Lancashire SRL in 1913. Before that, all inter-city/town matches were organised by the local associations, with the support of the Yorkshire section of the Northern Union, later to become the Yorkshire County Rugby League. In 1965, representatives from the Cumberland, Lancashire and Yorkshire associations got together to form the English Schools' Rugby League (a move first mooted four years earlier), with its first chairman being Fred Howarth of Oldham and the 'Objects' of the association being:

> *To foster the Physical, Mental, Social and Moral Development of the Schoolboys of England, in every type of school, through the medium of Rugby League Football.*
> *The formulation of expert opinion on coaching and methods of organisation.*
> *To promote inter-county competitions.*
> *To promote and organise inter-nation matches.*

Inter-county matches had been taking place since the 1920s, but the first 'inter-nation' match was played against France in Perpignan in 1967, with England victorious, 17-2. The squad was selected by each affiliated association putting forward one name; the Leeds representative was Philip Haller (Cross Green) and the Hunslet representative was Steven Evans (Belle Isle). This first international was played at Under 15 level; when the next game took place, in Hull in 1972, it was at Under 16 level. Again England won, this time just 5-2, and Leeds had representatives in Bryan Murrell (Stainbeck) and Martin Tate (St John Bosco).

From 1969-70, grants from the Rugby Football League were distributed by ESRL to local associations and, in the same season, one of the early achievements of ESRL was to prevent schoolboys playing in open age rugby league. At the time, Leeds & District ARL was the only league which already had a rule to prevent this happening.

ESRL grew to organise a number of inter-town and inter-school competitions from Under 11 to Under 16, but the only competition organised in the 1960s was the Under 15 ESRL Trophy.

Leeds City Boys Double

Over the 35 years of ESRL competitions, Wigan and Hull were the dominant associations in inter-town/city competitions, but in 1971 and 1972 Leeds completed a notable double by winning the ESRL Cup for two successive seasons, under the coaching of George Cranage and former Leeds winger Garry Hemingway, who taught for a number of years at Kirkstall Secondary (and later Middle) School.

Roy Dickinson, who led Wyther Park Junior School and

Benjamin Gott Secondary School to their only Leeds SRL honours, played in both victories. In 1971, when Leeds beat Hull, Dickinson's older teammates included future Leeds signings Bryan Murrell, Peter Judson, Martin Tate and Graham Jackson. While, in 1972, Sean Miller and a young Kevin Dick (who two years later would captain England Schools) were part of the side which beat Warrington.

It would be another 25 years before Leeds lifted the senior ESRL Cup again.

Record Participation as a New Era Dawns

The growth of junior school rugby and the broadening of the high school competitions to include all age levels meant that this era showed a healthy rise in the number of schools and teams playing the game, and the number of matches played.

More than 500 games were played during most seasons, contested by over 80 teams. There was great interest in the sport from pupils and teachers. In 1963, Leeds SRL secretary Bob Sheppard reported that a record 1473 handbooks had been sold that season, while £100 profit was made from the sale of the coaching manual 15 years after it had been first published. Upwards of 30 teachers often attended LSRL meetings; indeed the chairman *deplored the small attendance* at the 1965 AGM – 15 teachers.

Ten in attendance is a bumper crowd nowadays!

Two young teachers beginning their involvement in schools' rugby league at the end of the 1960s were John Ahm and Steve Bateson; both were to give long and distinguished service to the game. John started as George Cranage's protégé at Cross Green before following him to Clapgate Middle School where he built up his own excellent reputation as a coach there over the next 20 years, before moving on to

Matthew Murray. He served as a city and county coach, secretary of Hunslet & Morley SRL and Yorkshire, and was chair of Leeds, Leeds & Hunslet and the ESRL. He was also one of only two people to be elected as a life member of both the Hunslet and Leeds associations, and continued his work for the association until his sad passing in 2015. As well as for his work in schools' rugby league, John was much-respected in the community game (for his work with North Leeds Leopards) and at the Leeds Club (for his work as Kirkstall site manager and as club welfare officer).

Steve began his career in Middleton, moving soon to Raynville Primary; he coached successful sides at Royal Park Middle and continued through headship to coach teams at Greenhill and Holt Park Middle Schools and Farnley Park High. He served Leeds SRL as secretary for a total of 13 years (in two spells), was chair of Leeds (or Leeds & Hunslet) on four separate occasions and is currently president of the association. He is part of a unique family double as his father, Harold 'Ben' Bateson, also served as chairman of the association in the 1950s and 1960s.

Steve had the honour of refereeing the first Wembley Cup Final curtain-raiser, when he was in charge of the Under 11 match between Widnes and Wigan in 1975. He also officiated on the ESRL French Tour in 1978.

At meetings of the Hunslet and Leeds associations in 1971 and 1972, planning started for the changes to education in Leeds. With 16 soon to be established as the school leaving age for all, the introduction of middle schools would see another increase in the number of schools and teams playing schools' rugby league in the city.

THE ARCHIE GORDON GROUND

The Leeds Schools' Athletic Association
(later the Leeds Schools' Sports Association) purchased the
Thrift Stores Sports Ground in 1955.
The new ground was named after Archie Gordon, a retired headmaster,
former chairman of the LSAA and the founder of Leeds Children's Day,
who passed away shortly before its offical opening on 29th June 1956.
As well as providing sporting facilities for local schools,
it was, for many years, the home of Leeds Schools' Rugby League,
staging numerous cup finals and city boys' matches.
Its offical opening as a 3G pitch was on 5th December 2011.

Modern plaque to commemorate the opening of
the Archie Gordon Ground in 1956

Hunslet City Boys – Yorkshire Champions, 1957-58

Hunslet Carr – Lewthwaite Cup, Harrison Shield and
Jas Wilson Cup winners, 1957-58

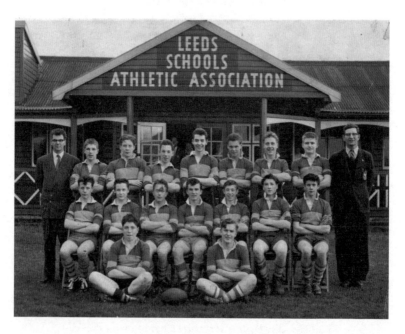

Leeds Senior City Boys, 1958-59

Middleton – Yorkshire Cup, Jas Wilson Cup,
Harrison Shield and Lewthwaite Cup winners, 1959-60

Leeds Intermediate City Boys, 1961-62

Harehills Under 14s – Jas Lyon Cup winners, 1962-63

Hunslet Senior City Boys – Yorkshire Champions, 1963-64

Leeds Intermediate City Boys, 1963-64

Burley Road – Long Trophy winners, 1964-65

Belle Isle – Lewthwaite Cup, Goldthorpe Cup (as intermediates),
Yorkshire Cup, Jas Wilson Cup and Harrison Shield winners, 1965-66

Leeds Senior City Boys, 1967-68

Leeds Senior City Boys, 1969-70

Leeds Senior City Boys – English SRL Cup winners, 1970-71

Steve Bateson referees the 1975 Wembley curtain-raiser

Clapgate Under 13s with all the trophies they won
over an unbeaten four-year period: 1974-78

5.
The Middle School Years
1972-1992

New Age-Levels, New Schools, New Areas

The 1970s was very much a golden decade for schools' rugby league in Leeds. Starting with the success of the Leeds City Boys in 1971 and 1972, the introduction of middle schools alongside ROSLA (Raising of the School Leaving Age to 16) saw an increase in the number of boys playing the game in organised competitions.

The age levels were extended from Under 9 through to Under 16 and rugby league was played in all tiers of statutory education. At the height of the decade, and into the 1980s, over 90 teams were in membership of Leeds schools' rugby league. Hunslet continued as a separate association for representative teams, but schools throughout the city combined for all league and most cup competitions.

A number of new names appeared in school competitions. Sometimes these were new names for old schools (Bewerley Street became Arthur Greenwood; Queen's

Road became Royal Park), schools playing for the first time following a change of designation (Clapgate Middle previously Clapgate Primary; Kirkstall Middle previously Kirkstall Secondary), or brand new schools created at reorganisation (Holt Park Middle and Thornhill Middle). In addition, schools from outside the traditional Leeds boundaries became part of the new Leeds Education Authority: Churwell, Gibson Lane (Kippax), Woodkirk, Brigshaw, Crawshaw, Bruntcliffe amongst many others.

As well as joining the Leeds competitions, some of these former West Riding Authority schools set up their own associations for competitions and representative sides. Morley established an autonomous association in 1975-76, the early driving forces being Ian Denton and Peter Dawson, supported by Churwell coach and headteacher Gerry Corfield and locally-based professional coach Maurice Bamford amongst others. The association ran various cup competitions at Under 11 and Under 10 as well as an Under 11 representative side. For the ten years that the association existed, the most successful school was Drighlington. The association combined with Hunslet in 1985, to become the Hunslet & Morley Schools' Rugby League. When this association in turn merged with Leeds in 1996, the name 'Morley' was lost from the title. Schools from the area, however, continued to support competitions in the city.

In 1982-83 there was an attempt to set up another new officially recognised association in the city: Airedale & Wharfedale District SRL. The area had long had its own sports association and for three years a successful seven-a-side rugby league tournament had been organised with the support of the Guiseley Rangers club, Brian Noble (then a local resident and player at Bradford Northern) and the ubiquitous Maurice Bamford. The driving force for recognition of a new association was Steve Ball, formerly a teacher in the area, then a teacher at John Blenkinsop and better-known later for his involvement at a number of professional clubs as well as being general manager of the Rugby League Benevolent Fund. The application to be a recognised association (for local primary school competitions, not for running a representative side) met with opposition from some areas of the county, but a one-year associate membership of Yorkshire Schools' Rugby League was granted for 1983-84. The impetus was lost however, and it wasn't until after 1995 that a primary school team from this area (Horsforth West End) entered Leeds competitions.

At the start of the 1970s most school games were played on a Saturday morning, with a fixture list for the season printed in the annual handbook. By the end of the decade an increasing number of matches took place after school: more representative games were arranged for Saturdays, high school boys had Saturday jobs and not as many teachers were keen to give up their Saturday mornings. Concerns were expressed as to the strength of high school rugby league in Leeds, but in middle and primary schools the game was flourishing.

High School Competitions Dominated by Two Names (But Just One School!)

After switching from rugby union to rugby league in the late 1960s, Parkside continued to be the team to beat in high school rugby league until well into the 1990s, the school closing down in 1999. The name change to Middleton Park, as the school changed site in 1983, had no effect on their success. They claimed over half the 100+ trophies to be won between 1972 and 1992. The Parkside years were led by Ken

Bond (who also coached some successful Hunslet city teams), ably supported by a number of other teacher-coaches including John Speight and John Ball, who continued into the Middleton Park era; while the 1980s saw the emergence of John Bedford, who also coached city and county Under 16 teams. The list of professional players to emerge from Parkside/Middleton Park is lengthy and includes Ian and Andrew Mackintosh, Andrew Mason, David Creasser, Garry Schofield, James Lowes, Daryl Cardiss, Marvin Golden and Wayne McDonald. Parkside completed a treble as Yorkshire Champions at Under 16 (1976-1978), and a double at Under 15 (1976 and 1977), while the school (as Parkside and as Middleton Park) reached Yorkshire finals in the 1980s and 1990s and also were twice runners-up in the Yorkshire 'Sevens'.

Cross Green won a couple of Leeds trophies and were Yorkshire Champions in 1974, but then faded from the honours board, despite the presence of well-respected city team and amateur coach Alan Hornby. Fifteen other schools won high school trophies in this era, but, to emphasise the Parkside/Middleton Park dominance, only two other schools won more than four trophies: Moor Grange (an all-boys school in Leeds 16) who had a couple of outstanding teams in the late 1970s coached by Under 16 city team coach Dougie Hainsworth, and Hough Side, a relatively small school in Swinnow, coached by one of schools' rugby league's real characters, Bill Hart. Remarkably they were Leeds Under 16 champions on three separate occasions and provided three players who graduated to the professional game: Gary Sidebottom, David Pitts and Paul Medley. Finally, a mention should be given to Harrington (formerly Cow Close, latterly Farnley Park) who were runners-up to Parkside in the 1976 Under 16 Yorkshire final.

New Trophies for Youngest Age-Group

While the new primary section of Leeds Schools' Rugby League rarely reached double figures of registered teams, a number of schools were stalwarts of the sport and, of course, many youngsters had their first taste of rugby league in primary schools. Registered primary schools played mainly monthly rallies on Saturday mornings at anything from 7-a-side to 13-a-side, depending on available numbers. In the early 1970s this Under 9 section included middle schools which had reorganised from primary and had age-groups still 'working their way through'. After a few seasons of rallies only, a couple of trophies were presented by the Bramley club, at 7-a-side (Tommy Callaghan Trophy, 1975-76) and at 13-a-side (Jim Windsor Cup, 1976-77).

The finals were played as curtain-raisers to Bramley matches at McLaren Field; well-received by players, staff and parents, as were the medals presented to the finalists – LSRL did not present anything to finalists of their competitions in those days.

In 1977-78, Hunslet SRL organised an Under 9 competition for the Culley Trophy, presented by John Morgan of the *Yorkshire Evening Post* and the family of John Culley who had been a Hunslet players between 1901 and 1906 and a lifelong supporter of the club until his death in 1973, aged 98. From 2002 a new version of the trophy would be used for the primary schools Under 11s' 7-a-side competition.

The first primary school trophy in 1975-76 was fittingly won by one of the oldest names in schools' rugby league, Hunslet Carr. After that, eight different seats of learning were amongst the honours, with the dominant schools being Bramley, Alwoodley and Churwell.

Middle Schools – The Flagship Age-Group

While many players learned their first rugby skills in primary school and some boys in Leeds high schools achieved the highest honours in the schoolboy game, the middle schools formed the strongest section of Leeds Schools' Rugby League during their existence from 1972 to 1992.

Many middle schools provided real strongholds of the game and helped league entries to rise from 70 teams in 1970-71 to a record 101 teams in 1978-79. Although it's true to say that in later years middle school leagues were bolstered by junior and high schools from the outer Leeds area, as well as Catholic schools that reorganised earlier, figures from 1991-92 (the last season of middle schools) show that over 70 per cent of registered teams were from middle schools.

The two most successful middle schools over the 20 years were Bramley C/E and Clapgate with 34 trophies each, with Holt Park in clear third place with 24. While Bramley's and Clapgate's honours were evenly spread through the years and through the age groups, Holt Park had an amazing haul of 15 trophies at Under 12 and won all but one of their trophies in the 1980s. Arthur Greenwood was the outstanding school in the early to mid-1970s, finishing as Under 13 champions for three successive years and winning the national Under 13 'Sevens' in 1975. Royal Park, Kirkstall and John Blenkinsop also produced a number of successful sides, as to a lesser extent did Intake and Braim Wood. Two names amongst the entries during most of the middle school years were Armley and Middlethorne; both enjoyed only rare trophy wins, but both played the game in an entertaining and sporting manner. Armley were served by a number of coaches who contributed well at different schools over the years, including Geoff Greenwood, Colin Trenholme, Tony Livesey, Peter Toepritz, Jeff Moore, Chris Ansell, Dave Tidman and Ric Brown. Middlethorne in contrast were well-served by a 'one-school' coach in Phil Pogson, who usually coached two teams each year. Altogether 27 different schools won middle school knockout cups or senior league trophies, with another 15 schools winning 'B' or 'C' league titles.

Despite the LSRL middle school leagues being the biggest competition in the country (in terms of number of teams) Leeds and Hunslet schools achieved very little success in individual school competitions at national and county level. Bramley C/E won the Under 12 Yorkshire Cup in 1991; Woodkirk were runners-up in the Under 12 Yorkshire final in 1987 and the Under 13 national final in 1988. Churwell were runners-up in the Under 11 national final in 1989 and were winners of the Yorkshire final in 1992 – they beat Kippax Gibson Lane, who were also runners-up in the national final in the same year; while Cross Hall (featuring future international Garreth Carvell) were county runners-up the previous year. As mentioned previously, Arthur Greenwood won the national Under 13 'Sevens' in 1975; the next year Royal Park finished as runners-up to St John Fisher of Dewsbury.

Supporters' Club Supports Schools

More than ten years after donating the Watson Trophy, the Leeds RL Supporters' Social Club donated two more trophies, named after prominent officials of the club. The Joe Wager Trophy (Under 12 knockout cup) in 1973-74 was followed by the Arthur Jewson Trophy (Under 14 knockout cup). In 1980-81 a fourth trophy was added, the Ken Lee Trophy, which was presented to the winners of the Under 13 League 'A'.

The History of Schools' RL in Leeds

Until well into the 1980s, the committee of the Supporters' Social Club staged individual presentation events for each of these trophies, where players were provided with engraved plaques and a late afternoon 'bun fight'. For a number of years the Supporters' Social Club were welcoming hosts for the end-of-season presentation evening, where trophies and city team badges were presented by players or officials from the Leeds Club. The concert room was packed with players, staff and families, and many future stars of the game can be spotted on photographs taken at the time.

John Featherstone, editor of the Leeds RL Supporters' Club handbook from 1974 to 1976, was keen to involve LSRL in the publication, featuring Leeds Under 11s' Wembley curtain-raiser, Parkside's Yorkshire Cup victory and the 'explosion' of junior rugby in west Leeds, as well as presentations of the above-mentioned trophies. In addition, all 14 editions of *Headingley Scene (the mouthpiece of the Headingley Grounds Branch of the Leeds Supporters' Club)* had a 'Schoolboy Rugby League' column.

LSRL press secretary Colin Trenholme performed an excellent job in securing regular coverage in the *Yorkshire Evening Post*, including photographs, match reports and features. Colin was also instrumental in introducing, from 1987-88, a certificate which would be presented to all future finalists in LSRL cup competitions; it was designed by Marc Gibson, Armley and Leeds City Under 13 player and later a stalwart of the Milford Club open-age team.

Another innovation during this era was the inauguration of the Ben Bateson Award. Named after a former chairman of the association, this trophy is awarded to a school or team for its sportsmanship and fair play, rather than necessarily for its success. The trophy was first awarded to Raynville Primary School in 1981-82; subsequently it was awarded to middle and high schools too, and in 1987-88 it was Broad Lane Middle School's first and only LSRL trophy.

There Were Tough Times Too

While the strong middle school section ensured high participation overall in Leeds, there were some problems emerging in the high school section. The LSRL committee meeting of 2nd April 1984 expressed concern that fewer games were being played than in previous seasons and *trophies are being won too easily*; indeed no Under 15 trophies were awarded that year. The following season, a mixture of bad weather and teacher action meant that only two teams completed their full programme of league fixtures. 1984-85 also saw the first move in the long-running saga of the sale of the Archie Gordon Ground. A couple of years later, the Leeds Schools' Sports Association (owners of the venue) agreed to its sale to Headingley Rugby Union Club for £150,000; LSRL officials at the meeting voted against the sale, which didn't go ahead anyhow, as Headingley soon began pursuing a move away from Kirkstall.

Continued teacher action meant severe disruption to the schools' rugby league programme in Leeds, and indeed in the rest of the north. In 1985-86 no league or knockout fixtures were played and no city teams were organised. The Under 14 cup final, held over from the previous season, was played in September, as were Headingley curtain-raisers for the Under 13 Wynne 'Sevens' Cup – the association did not want to lose this invitation from the Leeds club. Some teachers, depending on their union membership, continued to run teams which played 'friendlies' and where there was sufficient interest 'one-off' tournaments were organised at the end of the season at Under 9, Under 11, Under 12 and Under 13. This lack of action enabled BARLA junior teams to 'stake a claim' for Saturday mornings – a move from which schools' rugby league would never fully recover.

When the teacher action ended, entries for 1986-87 were 50 per cent of what they had been five years previously. There was a slight increase, particularly at high school level, over the next couple of seasons, but falling rolls, impending reorganisation and a lack of sufficient new teachers coming into the profession (as well as, of course, a hangover from the union action), meant that entries to competitions would never again reach the all-time highs of 1978-79 to 1980-81.

For the first time in 1980-81 an entry fee of £1 per team was charged; this was raised gradually to £5 by 1990-91. Schools could recoup this money by selling handbooks. From 1983-84 to 1996-97 these handbooks were well-produced, with a wealth of information and photographs, which was all excellent publicity for the association.

Representative Rugby

Leeds were Under 16 Yorkshire Champions in 1974 and Hunslet followed suit in 1977, when they were also national cup winners and champions of the recently inaugurated Under 16 national Division One. This was otherwise a barren period for the senior city sides, other than Hunslet winning the national second division in 1981, and Leeds doing likewise in 1984, after being runners-up in 1977 and 1982.

However, competitive representative schoolboy rugby league was extended to the Under 13 (1973-74, having played 'friendlies' since 1955-56) and the Under 11 (1975-76) age-groups, and Leeds teams enjoyed more success at these lower age-levels. At Under 13, Leeds completed a hat-trick of

Yorkshire Championship wins from 1983 to 1985, they were runners-up in 1988 and 1989, joint champions in 1990, before being champions again in 1991, when an outstanding team also won the English Schools' Rugby League Cup for the first time, beating Wigan in the final at Central Park, and triumphed in the Steve Mullaney invitation tournament. This event was organised by Wakefield SRL, in memory of one of their city players who died in a road accident only a year after a memorable try in the Wembley curtain-raiser, which is now named in his honour. Hunslet Under 13s were Yorkshire runners-up in 1985 and 1987; Leeds Under 13s were also national runners-up in 1984. Leeds were Under 11 Yorkshire Champions in 1976, 1987 and 1989, and runners-up in 1980; in addition they were national Division Two Champions in 1990.

Leeds and Hunslet schools provided a total of 20 players for the ESRL Under 16 national side during this period; they included Kevin Dick of Abbey Grange (who captained the 1974 England side), Ellery Hanley (Foxwood and Shadwell, 1977) and Vince Fawcett (Lawnswood, 1987) who would all go on to play for the Leeds first team, along with aforementioned Parkside and Hunslet City players Andrew Mason (1978), David Creasser and Garry Schofield (both 1981). Meanwhile schoolboy international Lee Child (Middleton Park, 1991) played in the Hunslet first team.

During this era there was a move to introduce competitive rugby league in sixth forms and colleges. Regional and national cups were held and a tour of Australia organised by BUSCARLA (British Upper Schools and Colleges Amateur Rugby League Association) in 1984. Leeds and Hunslet representatives were Mark Wilson (Airedale & Wharfedale College) and Mark Wood (Middleton Park School).

On The Big Stage

The first-ever Under 11 schools curtain-raiser to the Rugby League Challenge Cup final took place at Wembley in 1975.

Representative Under 11 rugby being more advanced in Lancashire, this first game was between Widnes and Wigan; the referee however was from Yorkshire: Stephen Bateson, at the time a teacher at Royal Park Middle School and secretary of Leeds Schools' Rugby League. Three years later Steve accompanied the ESRL Tour to France as referee and interpreter.

From 1977 until 1999, when 'development areas' were targeted, the curtain-raiser was traditionally Yorkshire versus Lancashire (or Cumbria), so in 1976, to restore the balance from the previous year, it was an all-Yorkshire affair, with Leeds playing Hull. The match was a 5-5 draw, but the result was incidental: as Leeds Under 11 captain Andrew Horner (Kirkstall) commented, ... *what a day to remember*!

The Leeds team included future Leeds first-teamers Norman Francis and Phil Owen. Hunslet Under 11s featured in the curtain-raiser in 1980, also contesting a 5-5 draw, against Warrington; in their team was future Bramley player Dean Creasser and future Hunslet players Alan Julian, Martin Rowse and Darren Webb. Two years later Morley lost to Wigan by 30 points to 5. Leeds' second visit came in 1987 when they were victorious against Warrington by 10 points to nil, prompting full back Mark Thomson (Fir Tree) to comment ... *we were on Cloud Nine for the rest of the time – in fact I don't think we came down for a few days*! The Leeds side included future Leeds first teamers Anthony and David Gibbons. St Peter's C/E headteacher and LSRL treasurer Peter Woodhead refereed the curtain-raiser in 1992, when he was in charge of a young Kevin Sinfield, as Oldham played Dewsury & Batley.

In 1983, Leeds Under 13s provided the ball boys for the Challenge Cup final; Kirkstall schoolboy David Francis completed a notable family double, as his brother Richard had played in the 1976 curtain-raiser. Hunslet Under 13s provided the ball boys in 1987.

For a number of years the Yorkshire County Rugby League had staged various curtain-raisers at their cup finals involving school teams; from 1976 they followed the RFL's lead in organising them initially at the youngest representative age-level. The first year's game was a repeat of the Wembley game with Leeds this time losing to Hull; the game was refereed by professional referee Trevor Court (who was also a teacher at Intake HS and then Abbey Grange). Out of the 17 years that the game was played (in later years at Under 13) there was involvement by teams and/or individuals from the City of Leeds in 13 of the years.

Morley lost to York in 1977; the referee was David Hall (Royal Park). Hunslet beat Wakefield in 1978 and in 1979 Leeds played Hull again, in a game refereed by Roy Dougill (Clapgate); Hunslet lost to Dewsbury & Batley in 1983; Morley played Huddersfield in 1984; Leeds lost to Wakefield in 1985, and Hunslet & Morley beat Hull in 1986. For the next few years LSRL provided the referee: Peter Woodhead in 1987 & 1988, Steve Boothroyd in 1989 and Steve Bateson in 1990. Then before the last ever Yorkshire Cup Final in 1992, Leeds Under 13s, including a young Andy Lynch, beat Hull 18-6. When Rodstock's 'War of the Roses' sponsorship revived the Yorkshire v Lancashire matches between 1985 and 1991, Yorkshire and Lancashire faced each other in an Under 12 clash (featuring the previous season's Under 11 sides).

Individual school teams also performed occasionally

on the 'big stage'. From 1980 to 1995, Under 13 school sides played in curtain-raisers at Headingley, contesting the semis and final of the Wynne 'Sevens' Competition. In 1980 Kirkstall MS Under 13s broke new ground by playing a representative team from London schools in a curtain-raiser to the Great Britain v New Zealand game at Headingley.

Although not appearing in front of such a large crowd, Braim Wood MS and later Holt Park MS also broke new ground by taking teams to play fixtures in London. Holt Park played a three-team tournament against Ambleside Avenue from Walton-on-Thames and (bizarrely!) Kirk Balk School from Barnsley, who were also 'on tour' in the capital.

One of the real stalwarts of schools' rugby league during this era was Brian Edmondson, who taught at Kirkstall School for its last couple of years as a secondary school and throughout its time as a middle school. As well as coaching his own school sides, he also coached at all levels of the representative game in Leeds, performed most of the organisational duties surrounding city teams, took charge of the Archie Gordon Ground and served as chairman of both Leeds SRL and Yorkshire SRL. Brian fully deserved the honour of leading out the Leeds Under 11s at Wembley in 1987.

With the closure of middle schools in 1992, decisions needed to be made as to the future structure of competitions. The challenge for Leeds Schools' Rugby League was to ensure that the kind of enthusiasm engendered by children and staff in middle schools could be maintained in the reorganisation of schools and school rugby league in the city.

6.
Changing Times
1992-2001

UNDER 13
1993-94

In an era that would see reorganisation and change, with merger and liaison continually on the agenda, it was fitting in the first season of the new era that Leeds Schools' Rugby League was invited, along with professional clubs, amateur clubs, junior clubs and women's teams, to be part of the Rugby League 7-a-side Challenge held at Headingley in May 1993, to celebrate the City of Leeds Centenary.

Clapgate beat Ralph Thoresby 8-6 in an exciting Under 11 clash. The event was organised by Damian McGrath, the city's rugby league development officer, previously a teacher-coach at Shakespeare Middle School, at the time a Batley player and later to become a highly-respected coach in both rugby league and rugby union.

Reorganisation and Merger

In the annual handbook in 1992, LSRL president Ron Pace noted that schoolboy rugby league in the city had been played now for 90 years, but that *the season 1992-93 is a new beginning; a new promise ... of a closer liaison between Schoolboy Rugby League and Leeds RLFC; new schools; new leagues and a new determination ... to make a great start.*

In the same handbook, H&MSRL chairman Ken Bond lamented the loss of middle schools, but looked forward to welcoming new or returning schools into competitions

Reorganisation did indeed bring new names, new schools and new coaches into competitions at all age levels. Some of these new schools had early success: Allerton and Ralph Thoresby won trophies and Temple Moor and Ireland Wood reached finals in the first couple of years of this era. Because of the uncertainty surrounding entries, strength of sides and the possibility of teams joining leagues part-way through the season, it was decided that all leagues should be run on a 'merit table' basis. Also, primary school rallies were to be held, with reduced numbers per side, to encourage new schools into the game.

It was envisaged that these arrangements would be just for one season, however leagues continued to be organised as merit tables, until high school leagues were abandoned for the 2000-01 season and the primary school system discontinued a year later. Understandably these first two seasons saw a reduction in the number of teams entering and matches played. However numbers increased steadily and by 1999 there were over 100 teams entered in competitions – the highest number for almost 20 years.

Due to changing competition structures, and also a growing number of different sports on offer in schools, the number of games played was not as high as during the 1970s and early 1980s. Nevertheless there was a very positive feel to rugby league in local schools by the end of this era. As well as teams playing inter-school games, a growing percentage of schools included rugby league on their curriculum. However, with the introduction of the National Curriculum and more demands on teachers' time, it did become harder to recruit volunteers to coach representative sides.

Hunslet & Morley had accepted Leeds boys into their Under 16 team since 1991 and in 1995 Hunslet & Morley boys were invited for trials with the Leeds Under 11 and Under 13 sides. With almost all competitions having been open to all schools in the city for a number of years, the next logical step was an official merger of the two associations.

After a few preliminary planning meetings, this took place at a meeting at the South Leeds Stadium on 10th June 1996. Seventy-five years, almost to the day, after the Hunslet breakaway, schools' rugby league in the city would again be organised by one single body. A narrow majority vote deemed that the association would be called Leeds & Hunslet Schools' Rugby League, rather than simply Leeds Schools' Rugby League.

Work to the pitch at the Archie Gordon Ground, and a lack of changing facilities, meant that the last 'big game' played at the venue had been the Under 14 Jewson Trophy final between Benton Park and Brigshaw on 4th April 1992. It would be more than eight years before L&HSRL would use this ground again. A number of different venues were used for City Boys trials, training and matches: the Arthur Thornton Ground (Hunslet SRL's traditional home), St Theresa's School, Headingley, West Leeds RUFC, Yarnbury RFC, Scott Hall Road fields and the Tetley's Sports Ground at Weetwood. Cup finals were held at Farnley Park School and later at Yarnbury, with Under 16 finals at Headingley and South Leeds Stadium.

After almost 80 years of meeting at Headingley, during refurbishments to the Supporters' Social Club, the LSRL committee moved to meet at the Vesper Gate public house and then the Yarnbury clubhouse for four years.

The same Leeds SRL AGM, in 1995, which set the wheels in motion for the merger with Hunslet & Morley a year later, also agreed that girls and boys could play together in mixed teams and that primary school competitions should be played to mod-league (11-a-side) rules.

These were certainly changing times.

Outward Shift

In 1993 Middleton Park were runners-up in the Under 16 Yorkshire Cup Final and shared the Under 16 Lewthwaite Cup with West Leeds for two successive seasons, but then their long 'dynasty' was over: with pupil numbers declining, the school finally closed in 1999.

Also in 1993 Bruntcliffe were Yorkshire Champions at Under 12 and they were to prove the most successful high school, with 21 league and knockout trophies during this era.

Bruntcliffe were just one of the schools which ensured the 'shift of power' to high schools outside the traditional Leeds (and Hunslet) boundaries: Woodkirk and Morley in the south, Brigshaw in the east and Crawshaw (who were runners-up in the 1995 Under 14 Yorkshire Cup final) and Grangefield in the west, all produced some successful teams. Inside the city, West Leeds and Merlyn Rees (formerly Belle Isle) provided strong opposition, while Intake, Cockburn and Braim Wood returned to trophy-winning days after long gaps (in Cockburn's case, almost 90 years!). West Leeds completed a hat-trick of senior championships in 1992-93, while Ralph Thoresby, Matthew Murray, Benton Park and Woodkirk were all senior league champions for the first time.

New Names on Primary School Trophies

The number of affiliated primary schools doubled during this era; a number of new schools and new teachers were attracted to the game and consequently a number of new names eventually found themselves amongst the honours.

For the first few years, however, most trophies were won by 'old names': Alwoodley, Clapgate (formerly middle now primary) and Churwell (who dominated at Under 10). All three schools also found success in the Yorkshire Cup: Alwoodley (runners-up in 1994), Churwell (runners-up in 1995) and Clapgate (winners in 1998 – the same year that they were runners-up in the last ever national Under 11 final). Bizarrely, however, the first primary league champions were actually from a high school, Ralph Thoresby, who, through the vagaries of reorganisation, had for a year an Under 11 side, which was basically the Holt Park MS side that had been Under 10 champions the previous year.

Nine-a-side rallies, 13-a-side and later 11-a-side league and cup competitions, along with local seven-a-side tournaments, all helped new players and new teams improve their skills in the sport. Cookridge, Middleton St Mary's, Hunslet St Mary's and St Augustine's all produced more than one trophy winning side, while in 1996-97 Iveson were league champions almost 30 years after the school's last trophy success.

Plenty of Success for Representative Sides

The committee of Leeds Schools' Rugby League started the 1993-94 season with plans for the revitalisation of the Under 11 and Under 13 Leeds City Boys Teams.

The initiative was driven by Colin Trenholme and Andrew Tidswell. An 'awareness-raising' committee was established, comprising teachers and parents, along with a 'patron' in current Leeds player (and former Clapgate, Middleton Park and Hunslet Schoolboy) James Lowes and LSRL vice-president Trevor Gibbons (ex-RL development officer in Leeds, now working for *Open Rugby* magazine). Guest coaches (including Australian 'guru' Frank Ponissi) were invited, a new sponsored kit was ordered, social evenings held, monthly newsletters distributed, increased publicity organised and season tickets provided for city boys by the Leeds Club.

Despite numerous changes in venue for training and matches, this new enthusiasm helped to make this era without doubt the most successful era for representative rugby in the city since the Leeds and Hunslet domination during the 1950s. Representative teams from the city won at least one county or national trophy every year from 1992 to 2001, and in 1996 the city completed a 'clean sweep' of the Yorkshire Championships. Admittedly the strength of teams was helped by the merger, but success began before that with Hunslet & Morley being county champions at Under 11 in 1993 and at Under 13 in 1994. At the same time Leeds Under 13s completed a hat-trick of appearances in the Steve Mullaney Memorial Trophy final (including two wins in 1992 and 1994). The city-wide Under 16 team, under the Hunslet & Morley banner, were Yorkshire Champions in 1994 and 1996, and began a rivalry with Wigan that would continue for the rest of this era – they beat Wigan to become national champions in 1994 and were runners-up to the same team in 1996.

As well as the Leeds and Hunslet merger, the 1996-97 season saw the launch of the English Schools' Rugby League

Under 16 Premiership competition, at the same time as the introduction of summer rugby. This was seen as a way of injecting new life into Under 16 rugby league with more city/town teams than ever in the competition. The Rugby Football League financed travel and honoraria paid to coaches, there was national sponsorship (through teachers' union NASUWT), local and national press coverage and the involvement of professional clubs who would provide facilities, coaching, playing kit and track-suits.

After a shaky start, the newly-named Leeds Rhinos certainly fulfilled their commitments, particularly with the valuable coaching of Tommy Gleeson and the expert knowledge of long-time SRL supporter (and former Middleton and Hunslet Schoolboy) Bob Pickles. Leeds & Hunslet's rivalry with Wigan continued: they beat the red-rose team in the 1997 and 1999 knockout finals, they were runners-up to the same team in the 1999 Premiership and then won the Premiership in its final year, 2000. Yorkshire SRL introduced an Under 15 knockout cup in 1997; Leeds & Hunslet dominated this competition, winning for four years out of the five it was contested (1997, 1998, 1999 and 2001). They also won the Dennis Davies Under 15 Cup (organised by the Manchester Referees' Society) in the last three of these years, having been runners-up in 1997.

The Leeds & Hunslet Under 13s won the ESRL Cup in 1997, beating St Helens, 22-6, in a memorable final at Headingley. The Under 13s were also runners-up (to Wigan) in the ESRL Championship for three successive years (1996-1998) and were Yorkshire Champions on four occasions (1996, 1997, 1998 and 2001). The Under 11s were runners-up in the ESRL Cup in 1995 and 1998 and in the ESRL Championship in 1998 and 1999; they were Yorkshire Champions on three occasions (1996, 1998 and 1999).

Amongst all this success, two long-serving representative coaches 'retired' on a high note in 1997. Steve Boothroyd had coached the Leeds Under 13s for over 10 years and had also coached county sides at Under 13; he continued to coach school sides and soon 'returned' as assistant coach of the Under 11 city team from 1998-2002. John Bedford had also coached at county level as well as enjoying much success as Under 16 city coach. He later became centre manager for the highly-respected *Playing for Success* study support initiative based at the Headingley Stadium.

A record number of Leeds and Hunslet boys represented county and national teams during this era, including future Leeds first team players Marvin Golden, Gavin Brown, Adam Hughes, Garreth Carvell, Karl Pratt, Jamie Jones-Buchanan, Andrew Kirk, Danny McGuire, Chev Walker, Richard Mathers, Ryan Bailey, Jonny Hepworth, Carl Ablett, Scott Murrell and Luke Gale, along with many more who made the grade at other professional clubs.

More Wembley Adventures

In 1994, Hunslet & Morley Under 11s were chosen to play in the Wembley curtain-raiser against Leigh. The Hunslet & Morley boys were well-beaten on the day, 26-0, but while none of the Leigh players progressed into the professional game, Hunslet & Morley provided two future Super League players in Chev Walker and Dwayne Barker, and a future Batley stalwart in Kris Lythe.

The Hunslet & Morley boys were coached by Don Horsfall (long-time coach at Belle Isle MS and then Cockburn HS) and had a memorable weekend as, on the Sunday after the game, they were invited to the Leeds Town Hall for a civic reception following the Leeds team's own appearance at Wembley. LSRL secretary Steve Boothroyd was nominated to referee the 1994 curtain-raiser and, in the same year, was chosen to referee the France versus England Under 16 international in Lézignan; he also refereed the international the following year in Hull.

The Leeds Under 11 team (comprising boys from all over the city as Hunslet & Morley no longer had a team) were selected to contest their third Wembley curtain-raiser in 1996, where they would face West Cumbria. Leeds maintained their unbeaten record at Wembley with an 18-6 victory; their side included a young Carl Ablett.

The Leeds association provided more cup final curtain-raiser referees than any other association; David Tidman refereed the Hull v Salford game in 1998 and Peter Todd was in charge of the Dublin v Gateshead match in 1999.

Girls Make Their Mark

Former Leeds City Boys coach David Warburton had created controversy in 1989 when he included a girl, Natasha Weekes, in his Hunslet C/E Under 11 school team. The matter was discussed by LSRL and prompted press coverage at the time, before *education chiefs* in Leeds City Council banned mixed rugby league because of possible *sexual impropriety*; it was also suggested that *there are clear anatomical risks to young women and the games could cause emotional problems*.

Girls were definitely interested in playing the game in school, however, and the first girls' tournament for junior schools in Morley was held on 24th April 1991 and attracted 12 teams, playing full-contact rules. After reorganisation primary schools from other areas of the city took part and the tournament continued until 1996. By this time there had been national controversy with regard to the inclusion of Sophie

The History of Schools' RL in Leeds

Cox in Rochdale Schools' Under 11 squad to play at Wembley in 1993. Media and political pressure meant that this happened, despite the disapproval of ESRL; while the Leeds City Council stance was that girls could play rugby in school, but tackling should be omitted. Finally, with a rule change driven by Iveson PS teacher Alun Davies, it was agreed at the 1995 AGM that boys and girls could play together in mixed teams. Many girls began to appear in primary school teams and certainly began to make their mark in the game. Girls appeared in both teams which contested the 1996 Under 11 Watson Trophy Final: Gemma McDowell of Middleton St Mary's (who had appeared first in the Crowther Cup final) and Claire Frost and Donna Holmes, who were both try-scorers for Seven Hills, in the school's first and only cup final success.

The End of Leagues and Representative Schools' RL

Although the number of teams affiliated to the association had increased through the 1990s, the number of fixtures played by each team had decreased to the point where the committee of L&HSRL decided to abandon the league structure in high schools for 2000-2001 and in primary schools for 2001-2002. The future structure for high schools would be 13-a-side rallies, 13-a-side cup competitions and 7-a-side tournaments. For primary schools it would be 9-a-side rallies, 11-a-side cup competitions and a 7-a-side tournament. In 2000-2001 the first school to be crowned senior champions solely by knockout cup was Grangefield, while the last primary school league champions were Cookridge.

During this era the structure for county and regional matches was changed by ESRL (under RFL influence). In 1997-98 Leeds & Hunslet became part of West Yorkshire, playing county matches against East Yorkshire and the South (including Wales); these 'counties' then combined to form South & East, which played regional games against North & West. For two years (1999 and 2000) the national team was known as Great Britain & Ireland SRL (there was an avenue for Welsh boys to gain selection, but the team remained all-English). Despite RFL's big promotion of the ESRL Premiership in 1996, there was soon a move to dismantle school representative rugby league, despite resistance from ESRL. The international was moved to Under 15 for 2000-2001, so the Under 16 tournament was now unimportant and all ESRL national tournaments were abandoned during this season. County competitions remained, but for 2001-2002 the RFL decided that representative schools' RL was not part of their policy.

Some associations in Lancashire defied this ruling for a couple of years, particularly at Under 11, and the last representative match played by L&HSRL was against Widnes Under 11s on their Easter Tour in 2002. The Leeds & Hunslet side was selected from boys playing regularly in school teams and a few players who played a year under-age for the previous year's Under 11 side; the side included future Hunslet players Brooke Broughton and Aston Wilson. The match was drawn 18-18, described in the minute book as *an excellent performance and an excellent occasion.*

Into The Next Millennium

While there were negative aspects to some of the changes during this era, there were plenty of positive developments to enjoy and to look forward to, many due to closer liaison with the Leeds Club and local amateur clubs.

Brought about by the then Leeds coach Doug

The History of Schools' RL in Leeds

Laughton's first promise of club involvement and the introduction of the 'Leeds Niners', through Ken Bond's work with the 'apprentices' at Headingley, Julia Lee's work as Leeds City Council RL development officer to build bridges with the amateur game and promote girls RL, Paul Fletcher's and Damian McGrath's work in school/club liaison, the introduction of the 'classroom' at Headingley, financial support from the Leeds Ex-Players Association, to, above all, Gary Hetherington's great determination to provide opportunities and support for rugby league in schools; there was much to look forward to as schools' rugby league in Leeds entered a new millennium and anticipated its own centenary.

Leeds Under 11 City Boys, 1980-81, pictured with deputy mayor
Councillor Denise Atkinson and LSRL president W H 'George' Hirst

Parkside School – Lewthwaite and Jas Wilson Cup winners, 1981-82

Holt Park Under 13s – Wynne 'Sevens' winners, 1982-83, along with
Meeks Shield, Wynne Trophy and Wager Trophy (all won as Under 12s)

Holt Park Under 12s – presented with the Llewellyn 'Sevens' Trophy
by RFL Secretary, David Oxley, 1983-84

Leeds Under 13 City Boys, 1983-84

Leeds SRL Presentation Evening 1984, with special guest
Leeds coach Maurice Bamford

Leeds Under 13 City Boys – Yorkshire 'Sevens' winners, 1984-85

Hough Side Under 15s – Ben Bateson Award,
league and cup winners, 1986-87

Leeds Under 11 City Boys after the Wembley curtain-raiser, 1987

Leeds Under 13 City Boys, 1986-87

Leeds SRL Presentation Evening 1988, with special guest David Creasser
(Leeds player and former Hunslet City Boy)

Leeds Under 13 City Boys – ESRL Cup and
Steven Mullaney Memorial Trophy winners, 1990-91

Leeds Under 13 City Boys – after the Yorkshire Cup final
curtain-raiser, 1992

Bruntcliffe Under 12s – Yorkshire Champions, 1992-93

Leeds Under 13 City Boys –
Steven Mullaney Memorial Trophy finalists, 1993

Hunslet & Morley Under 11 City Boys
after the Wembley curtain-raiser, 1994

7.
A New Millennium –
Rugby League For All
2001 onwards

There was a great optimism surrounding the involvement of the Leeds Rhinos club as the association moved into the 21st century. The Leeds Rugby Foundation (later the Leeds Rhinos Foundation) began to take rugby league into a growing number of schools; the girls' game really took off and, working with Leeds City Council, the Foundation hosted disability tag rugby festivals at South Leeds Stadium and Headingley.

As pressures on teachers' time increased and it became more difficult to organise training and matches after school, fewer serving teachers were willing to commit themselves to organising anything other than their own school sides. The Foundation gradually took on more and more of the roles previously held by teachers and the L&HSRL Committee. Currently members of the Foundation work closely with the committee and a wider range of opportunities are available to schools and schoolchildren, while the traditions and ethos of the association are maintained.

Centenary Celebrations

A century of schools' rugby league in Leeds was celebrated in 2002-2003. The committee reflected on the wealth of changes since the Leeds Schools' Rugby Football Union was officially formed in September 1903, after the association's first season, and worked closely with the Leeds Club to organise two special events.

On 14th November 2002 a *Centennial Dinner* was held in the Executive Suite at Headingley. Ron Pace (president, L&HSRL) and Steve Boothroyd (Chair, L&HSRL) performed the welcome and introductions, while the speakers were Harry Jepson OBE (past secretary of Hunslet RLFC, past director Leeds RLFC and former Leeds schoolteacher) and John Boyd (BBC radio and television). A number of current and past teacher-coaches were present at the event, including Ken Bond, who was soon to retire after 11 years managing the apprenticeship scheme.

On 7th June 2003 Merlyn Rees beat West Leeds in the *Centenary Cup Final* played as a curtain-raiser to the Leeds v Castleford Super League fixture. Past schoolboy representative players and coaches were invited to parade around the pitch at half-time and enjoy a meal in the Long Bar after the game. A *Board of Attendance* was produced and erected in the Leeds Supporters' Social Club.

Leeds Rhinos Foundation

As we enter the third decade of the century, the fact that so many schools in Leeds are playing rugby league is, without doubt, due to the ever-increasing work of the Leeds Rhinos Foundation. The year 1997 saw the beginnings of some community development work, as well as more regular matchday involvement for schools; 2000 saw Bob Pickles appointed by the Leeds Club as the first Schools' Liaison Officer; 2001-02 saw support from the Leeds Ex-Players Association, which purchased medals and equipment for L&HSRL. However, it was the establishing of the Leeds Rugby Foundation in 2005, along with the Foundation's first development plan in 2007-08, which ensured the long-term, coordinated support of schools' rugby league in the city. Members of the Foundation have regularly attended committee meetings since 2007.

A name change to the Leeds Rhinos Foundation took place in 2014. The Foundation works in the community in the areas of sport, health, the arts, heritage and education. Its work with schools includes assemblies, health education, mental health, attendance, dance and multi-sports, as well as curriculum coaching and after-school clubs. Gradually the Foundation has also taken on the organisation of the traditional L&HSRL competitions, as well as the introduction of new competitions in the areas of girls' rugby, tag rugby and the *Sky Try* nines for boys. A number of staff from the Foundation have championed the cause of schools' rugby league, none more so than former city boy Jonny Wainhouse and current competitions coordinators Ian Hardman and Lois Forsell. The Hunslet Hawks club (as it then was) and, from 2014, the Hunslet Rugby Foundation, have also done some valuable development work in south Leeds.

Local Competitions

Over the last 19 years, 14 different schools have been crowned senior champions, with just Bruntcliffe (four times), and Lawnswood, Rodillian and Brigshaw (twice each), taking the title more than once. One notable winner was Leeds Grammar School in 2012-13, after claiming their first ever trophy, at Under 14, two years earlier. A further eight schools have been among the cup honours in younger high school age-groups. During this era, high school cup winners at all age-levels have been decided in three different ways: (1) a knockout cup, (2) rallies and play-offs and (3) leagues and play-offs. For the first decade, Rodillian were the most successful school over all the age groups, while in recent years Corpus Christi and Brigshaw have dominated the finals. As well as the traditional L&HSRL trophies – which until 2010 included seven-a-side and then nine-a-side competitions – the Leeds Rhinos Foundation have since 2015 organised Plate competitions for Years 7-11 and the *Sky Try* Nines Competition for Years 7, 8 and 9.

The traditional primary school competitions – Watson (Under 11) Trophy, Burton (Under 10) Trophy and the Culley 'Sevens' Trophy – have continued to be contested each year. Over 50 different schools have entered competitions over the years, but interest has varied with staff leaving and joining schools, and fewer than half this number have entered competitions in any one year. Immaculate Heart completed a clean sweep of trophies in 2005-06 and Highfield repeated this feat in 2016-17.

Altogether 22 different schools have won at least one trophy; Alwoodley having been the most successful with 10 wins until the retirement of Neil Key, who probably achieved a record by coaching sides at the same school for 37 years. The hard work of the Foundation, Sports Partnerships and the City Council ensure a large number of primary schools support city-wide tag rugby tournaments.

Champion Schools

In 2003, the Rugby Football League took over the ESRL Champion Schools competition, re-organising, re-branding and re-launching it with great success that would see it grow into the world's largest junior rugby league tournament. Locally organised competitions, led to centrally organised county or regional tournaments and then to a national tournament.

The Under 12 final would be played as a curtain-raiser to the Rugby League Challenge Cup final, the other finals would be played at a venue close by, the day before. L&HSRL had a big involvement in these first finals: Alun Davies refereed the Cup final curtain-raiser, Peter Todd was also involved in the officiating and Steve Boothroyd (as ESRL chairman) was part of the presentation party. However it was not until 2010 that a Leeds school reached the final: Temple Moor were runners-up in the Under 12s and the team repeated this feat as Under 13s and Under 14s.

South Leeds were runners-up as Under 12s and Under 13s in 2011 and 2012, Priesthorpe Under 14s were runners-up also in 2011, Bruntcliffe Under 15s were runners-up in 2013 and Corpus Christi Under 13s runners-up in 2018. As might be expected, Leeds schools had more success in the Yorkshire Cup, with the following winning sides: Morley (Under 13 – 2002), West Leeds (Under 15 - 2003), Temple Moor (Under 13 – 2011), South Leeds (Under 12 – 2011), Temple Moor (Under 14 – 2012), Brigshaw (Under 16 – 2018) and Corpus Christi (Under 13 – 2019).

The RFL introduced a Girls' Champion Schools tournament in 2004, commencing with Under 12s only and building up to include Under 16s by 2008. It was the girls' competition which provided Leeds with its first national champions, when Corpus Christi Under 12s won the final at Victory Park, Warrington, in 2018. The team then repeated this feat as Under 13s the following year. Corpus Christi had also been the first Leeds girls' team to win the Yorkshire Cup, when their Under 14s were victorious in 2014, while both their Under 12 and Under 13 teams were Yorkshire Champions in 2018, as were the Under 13s again in 2019.

The Growth of Girls' Rugby League

For ten years the organisation and development of girls' rugby league in Leeds schools was rather ad hoc, very dependent on staff interest.

In 2005-2006 a primary school 'tag' rugby tournament was organised by the Leeds West Partnership and the Leeds Rugby Foundation, with L&HSRL providing a shield; but after three years it failed to attract sufficient entries. It was 2017 before the shield was contested again, as a full-contact competition to run alongside the 'tag' rugby tournament which the Leeds Rhinos Foundation began again in 2013.

The Champion Schools tournament was, unsurprisingly, a catalyst for a growth in high schools: Bruntcliffe and Matthew Murray played in the first county festival, Bruntcliffe Under 13s won the first Jane Tomlinson Trophy in 2007-08 and 'War of the Roses' games were played against Wigan schools. A lot of good work was done by Laura Clarke of the Leeds Rugby Foundation, but it wasn't until Lois Forsell joined the Foundation in 2013 that a regular programme of coaching and competitions (tag and contact) was developed.

A growing number of schools are now promoting girls' rugby league and organising teams. Corpus Christi have grabbed all the headlines in the girls' game in 2018 and 2019, but locally Allerton, Crawshaw, Temple Moor, Cardinal Heenan, Benton Park, Bishop Young and Ralph Thoresby have also won local honours recently, while Royds (Under 13 – 2012), Temple Moor (Under 13 – 2015) and Mount St Mary's (Under 12 – 2015) have all been runners-up in the Yorkshire Cup.

In recent years primary school competitions have been dominated by Shadwell (tag) and Woodlesford (contact).

With the recently-launched Women's Super League and a Leeds Rhinos women's side, schoolgirls in Leeds now have a high-profile team to aspire to. Some girls who played at high school have already progressed into the team, while experienced forward Danika Priim began her rugby league career at Cookridge Primary School.

Representative Rugby

Service Area sides replaced city/town teams in 2001-2002, club and school coaches being involved in all the sides in Leeds. Service Area rugby never commanded the high profile of schools representative rugby and was soon axed by the RFL. Since then the pathway for elite players has been coaching camps and professional club scholarships. Foundation, school and club coaches combined to organise North v South fixtures in Leeds at Under 13 and Under 14, but these matches did not receive RFL approval.

The Under 16 national side continued to be branded as 'English Schools' until 2009; the last Leeds & Hunslet Schoolboy to come through the local representative side and play for the England side was Ryan Gaunt, who played half-back for the Under 11s in 2001 and 2002 and represented the Under 16 national side as hooker in 2007.

Two primary school girls' sides representing the City

of Leeds, organised jointly by the Service Area and L&HSRL, played in the West Yorkshire Games in 2004.

Amongst The Honours

To celebrate the memory of long-serving teacher and committee member, John Ahm, who passed away in 2015, an award was introduced for high schools. Mirroring the Ben Bateson Award (which is now open only to primary schools), it is presented to a school or a team for sportsmanship and effort, rather than necessarily for success. The first winners were Abbey Grange.

In 2014, Lee Parkin (John Smeaton) was selected as ESRL Teacher of the Year; James Endersby was nominated for the same award in 2018, the year his Corpus Christi Year 7 girls' team were chosen as ESRL Girls' Team of the Year. The following individuals and teams have been recognised at the Leeds Sports Awards: Madeleine Hegarty, Sports Volunteer of the Year, 2012; John Ahm, Outstanding Services to Sport, 2014; Brigshaw Year 11 Boys, Young Club/Team of the Year 2017; Corpus Christi Year 7 Girls, Young Club/Team of the Year, 2018; Charlie Pyatt and Steve Boothroyd, Service to PE and School Sport, 2018. In addition Steve Boothroyd received the John Holmes Memorial Award, from Leeds Rugby Foundation in 2014, for Services to Rugby League in the city.

Finally, two rugby league players, who began their careers in the school game, were the first two winners of the accolade 'The Fastest Man in Rugby League': Leeds' Jamel Chisholm (Blenheim PS and Lawnswood HS) won in 2009 and 2010, succeeded in 2011 by Salford's Jodie Broughton (Ireland Wood PS, Ralph Thoresby HS and Leeds & Hunslet City Boys).

The Future

As the second decade of the new millennium begins, Leeds & Hunslet Schools' Rugby League's partnership with the Leeds club is as strong as ever. A small committee, under chairman David Pattison, continues to maintain the long traditions of the association and is currently striving to recruit younger members.

Through the work of the Leeds Rhinos Foundation more schools than ever are playing rugby league and have access to many other benefits in education, health and sport.

At the time of writing, nobody knows what long-term effect the coronavirus pandemic will have on rugby league in schools and indeed game-wide; however the whole of the game is looking forward to the Rugby League World Cup, planned to be held in England in October and November 2021.

Hopefully the legacy of this competition will benefit all areas of the sport, including schools' rugby league in Leeds.

Woodkirk Under 13s – Ben Bateson Award winners, 1994-95

Action from one of the first girls' tournaments in Morley, 1995

Leeds Under 11 City Boys after the Wembley curtain-raiser, 1996

Iveson Primary School – Hirst Trophy and
Iveson 'Sevens' winners, 1996-97

Leeds & Hunslet Under 13 City Boys – ESRL Cup winners, 1996-97

Leeds & Hunslet Under 16 City Boys – ESRL Cup winners, 1998-99

Blenheim Primary School – Culley 'Sevens' finalists, 2004

Players display the primary school girls' tag rugby shield
and the Super League trophy, 2008

Adel and Alwoodley share the Culley primary school
seven-a-side trophy, 2012

Bruntcliffe Year 11 – Lewthwaite Cup winners, 2011-12

Crawshaw Year 9 – Harrison Shield winners, 2017-18

Corpus Christi Year 8 – first winners of the girls'
Goldthorpe Cup, 2017-18

Corpus Christi Year 7 – National Champions, 2017-18

Cockburn Year 8 – L&HSRL Plate winners, 2018-19

Corpus Christi Year 8 – Yorkshire Champions, 2018-19

Farnley Year 8 – Goldthorpe Cup winners, 2019-20

Acknowledgements

The inspiration to research and write this brief history of schools' rugby league has come from the teachers who have driven the game through the years, past colleagues who encouraged me in my early involvement, current colleagues who continue to support the game, and of course the many hundreds of boys and girls, in school and representative sides, who have responded so well to my coaching, cajoling and complimenting – not forgetting a similar number of parents who have supported their children's efforts in so many ways.

A special thank you is given to the many people who have helped with my research in person, by email or through social media.

Photographs have come from a variety of sources and eras, which makes acknowledgement extremely difficult. If any copyright has been breached, it is entirely unintentional.

The History of Schools' RL in Leeds

The photograph of St Simon's, 1951-52, is by kind permission of Leeds Libraries, www.leodis.net. Other photographs are included by kind permission of:

Michael Minikin Photography
Hunslet Parkside Rugby League Ex-Players Group
(Facebook Group)
Leeds & District Amateur Rugby League Heritage
(Facebook Group)
Leeds Rhinos Foundation (Facebook page, Twitter account)
Laurie Baker
Phil Holmes
Steven and Susan Lee
Ernest Lundy
Stephen McGrail
(www.albertgoldthorpe.info/goldthorpe_cup.htm)
Nicky McGuire
Les Marshall
Bob Pickles
Bernard Shooman
The family of Donald Simpson

To complement the narrative of this history, a list of trophy winners from 1902 to the present day, along with other information about the school game in Leeds, Yorkshire and nationally, can be found on the official Leeds & Hunslet Schools' Rugby League website:
https://leedsandhunsletsrl.wixsite.com/mysite-4

Finally, grateful thanks are due to Phil Caplan for his support and valuable advice.

Steve Boothroyd
June 2021

 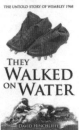 

At the outset of a glorious and varied career, Bev Risman faced two major dilemmas.

Should he represent his ancestral homeland Wales or England, his country of birth? Ought he to play rugby league or rugby union?

Son of league icon Gus, Risman made his name in the fifteen-a-side code, playing for England and touring with the 1959 British Lions.

After initially moving to rugby league with Leigh, he enjoyed huge success at Leeds, with whom he played in the famous Watersplash Challenge Cup final.

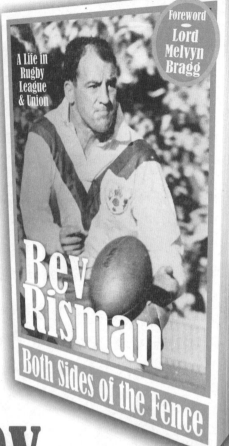

A Life in Rugby League & Union

Foreword Lord Melvyn Bragg

Bev Risman

Both Sides of the Fence

Rugby dynasty and destiny

With a foreword by Lord Melvyn Bragg, *Both Sides of the Fence* offers insight into decades of great change. A fascinating autobiography, it lays open the events and personalities that dominated both codes of rugby.

"A highly readable memoir..."
The Guardian

Be inspired.

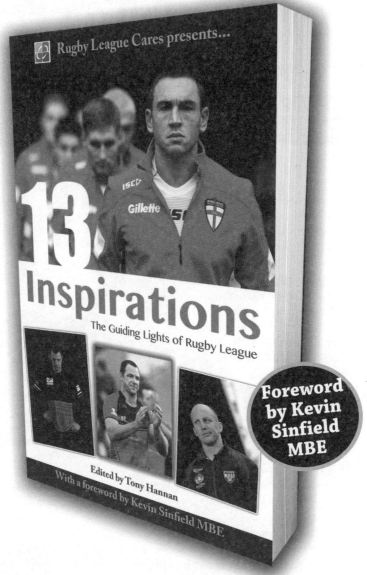

With contributions from many of the leading writers and
personalities in the game, **13 Inspirations** is a lively literary
collection in praise of the guiding lights of rugby league.

In aid of Rugby League Cares

Learning Curve

The Remarkable Story of Student League

Dave Hadfield

Learning Curve - Dave Hadfield's seventh book about rugby league - is devoted to one of the game's great untold stories.

The history of Student rugby league is marked by the defiance of prejudice and obstruction in building one of the code's most thriving sectors. Kicking off with the pioneers of the 1960s Hadfield traces the birth of the game in universities and colleges. From the founding fathers at Portsmouth and Leeds, he has gleaned the heroic truth behind those early years.

The spread of Student rugby league throughout England is highlighted by chapters on league development at Oxford and Cambridge - where sceptics said it would never penetrate.

From dozens of interviews with the most closely involved, alongside the author's inimitable observations of the state of play today, rugby league's best-loved writer captures the spirit of one of the sport's great successes - from the dedication at the elite level to humour in the lower echelons. Whether you played at university or college or not, *Learning Curve* is an unmissable read for those interested in the future of rugby.

www.scratchingshedpublishing.com

"Schools rugby league is the lifeblood of the game..." Neil Fox MBE

DIFFERENT CLASS

The Story of Schools Rugby League

Around the turn of the 20th century, schools rugby league was formalised. Compiled from a nationwide archive, *Different Class* puts a long and illustrious history in context, capturing its flavour with an array of colourful contributions.

Examining the communities from which it sprang, neighbourhood rivalries, prevailing social conditions, stories of overcoming great odds and trips into the unknown, it traces the pioneering spirit that has characterised the schools game, and the role played by teachers as mentors and inspiring personalities. Mixing fact and anecdote, the book contains a wealth of reminiscences from some who went on to become superstars of the sport, alongside those for whom the school playing field was their zenith.

DIFFERENT CLASS

The Story of Schools Rugby League

Phil Caplan ● Ron England

Phil Caplan ● Ron England

www.scratchingshedpublishing.com

Investigate all our other titles and
stay up to date with our latest releases at
www.scratchingshedpublishing.co.uk